The Countries

Nepal

Kate A. Conley

ABDO Publishing Company

visit us at
www.abdopub.com

Published by ABDO Publishing Company, 4940 Viking Drive, Edina, Minnesota 55435.
Copyright © 2004 by Abdo Consulting Group, Inc. International copyrights reserved in
all countries. No part of this book may be reproduced in any form without written
permission from the publisher.

Printed in the United States.

Photo Credits: AP/Wide World p. 32; Corbis pp. 5, 6, 9, 10, 14, 16, 17, 18, 19, 20,
    21, 23, 24, 26, 27, 29, 30, 31, 34, 35, 36, 37; Getty Images pp. 11, 33

Editors: Stephanie Hedlund, Kristianne E. Vieregger
Art Direction & Maps: Neil Klinepier

Library of Congress Cataloging-in-Publication Data

Conley, Kate A., 1977-
    Nepal / Kate A. Conley.
        p. cm. -- (The countries)
    Includes index.
    Contents: Namaste! -- Fast facts -- Timeline -- The kingdom of Nepal -- Nepal's land --
Forests & flowers -- Saving the animals -- The Nepali people -- A nation of farmers --
Old city, new city -- From here to there -- Nepal's government -- Land of festivals --
Nepali culture.
    ISBN 1-59197-293-0
    1. Nepal--Juvenile literature. [1. Nepal.] I. Title. II. Series.

DS495.5.C63 2003
954.96--dc21

                                                        2003040334

Contents

Namaste!

Hello from Nepal! For many years, Nepal **isolated** itself from other nations. Then in 1951, the country opened its borders. Today, people from across the globe are discovering this charming nation.

Visitors to Nepal are often impressed with its beautiful land. The country has a vast area of lowland that leads to hills and valleys. In turn, they give way to the world's highest mountain, Mount Everest.

Nepal is also home to amazing religious artwork. Ancient **Hindu** and **Buddhist** monuments and sculptures are common throughout the country. These works of art are a part of everyday life.

Nepal's history as a nation has been long and difficult. Over time, ancient kingdoms gave way to a modern government. Today, Nepal faces many challenges as it begins the twenty-first century.

Namaste *from Nepal!*

Fast Facts

OFFICIAL NAME: Kingdom of Nepal (Nepal Adhirajya)
CAPITAL: Kathmandu

LAND
- Area: 54,363 square miles (140,800 sq km)
- Mountain Ranges: Great Himalaya, Siwalik, and Mahabharat Ranges
- Highest Point: Mount Everest 29,035 feet (8,850 m)
- Major Rivers: Kosi, Gandak, and Karnali Rivers

PEOPLE
- Population: 25,873,917 (July 2002 est.)
- Major Cities: Kathmandu, Lalitpur, Bhaktapur
- Language: Nepali (official)
- Religions: Hinduism, Buddhism, Islam

GOVERNMENT
- Form: Parliamentary democracy and constitutional monarchy
- Head of State: King
- Head of Government: Prime minister
- Legislature: Parliament
- Nationhood: 1769

ECONOMY
- Agricultural Products: Rice, corn, wheat, sugarcane, root crops; milk; buffalo meat
- Manufactured Products: Food goods, brick, tile, paper, cement, rugs
- Money: Nepalese rupee (1 rupee = 100 paisa)

KATHMANDU

Nepal's flag

Nepali man counting rupee in collection plate

Timeline

1769	Prithvi Narayan Shah founds the modern nation of Nepal
1846	Jung Bahadur leads a coup and gains power as Nepal's prime minister
1940s	Nepali overthrow government and restore monarchy
1959	Nepal holds its first election
1960	King Mahendra dismisses the government, bans political parties, and seizes control of Nepal
1990	King Birendra lifts the ban on political parties and takes a less active role in the government
2001	Nepal's king and queen are murdered by their son, and the nation faces instability
2002	King Gyanendra dismisses government and appoints a prime minister until next election

The Kingdom of Nepal

Nepal's earliest kingdoms ruled the valley near the city of Kathmandu (kat-man-DOO). Over many years, several **dynasties** ruled this area. Then in 1769, a man named Prithvi Narayan Shah (PRIHT-vee nuh-RAH-yahn SHAH) conquered the valley.

Shah's **conquest** marked the beginning of the modern nation of Nepal. He made Kathmandu the kingdom's capital. From there, he and his successors expanded the kingdom's borders.

In 1846, a nobleman named Jung Bahadur (JUHNG buh-HAH-dur) led a **coup**. After the coup, a king from the Shah family remained in power. Bahadur, however, became Nepal's **prime minister**. As prime minister, he had more power than the king.

Bahadur later adopted the title Rana. The Rana family became powerful in Nepal. For more than 100 years, all of Nepal's **prime ministers** were part of this family.

Many dynasties ruled this area of Nepal, which is called Kathmandu Valley.

King Mahendra

By the late 1940s, the Nepali (nuh-PAW-lee) were discontented with the Rana family controlling the country. So, the Nepali overthrew the government and restored the **monarchy**.

In 1959, Nepal held its first election. However, Nepal's King Mahendra (muh-HAYN-druh) disliked the fighting among the political parties. So in 1960, he dismissed the government and banned political parties. A new **constitution** gave the king more power.

For the next 30 years, kings ruled Nepal. However, Nepali protested. They wanted to end the ban on political parties. In 1990, King Birendra (bee-REHN-drah) lifted the ban and accepted a less powerful role.

Despite this, Nepal still faces challenges. The government is unstable. In 1996, **communist rebels** began attacking Nepal. And in 2001, King Birendra and Queen Aishwarya (eye-sh-WAHR-ee-ah) were murdered by their son.

King Birendra's brother Gyanendra (gyah-NEHN-dreh) became king. In October 2002, King Gyanendra dismissed the elected government. He appointed a **prime minister** until new elections could be held.

Today, Nepali are hopeful that order will soon return to their country. They look forward to a stable government and peace with the communist rebels.

King Gyanendra

Nepal's Land

Nepal is located in southern Asia. Nepal's neighbor to the south, west, and east is India. Along the north, Nepal borders Tibet (tuh-BEHT), which is a region in China.

The land in Nepal can be divided into three regions. They are the Terai (tuh-RI) the Inner Terai, and the Mountain Region. Each region stretches from east to west.

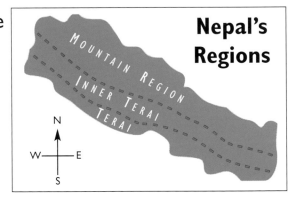

Nepal's Regions

The Terai is located along Nepal's southern border. This region has rich farmland. Some parts of the Terai are also marshy.

The Inner Terai lies in central Nepal. It is located between the Siwalik and Mahabharat Mountain Ranges. Land in the Inner Terai has hills and valleys.

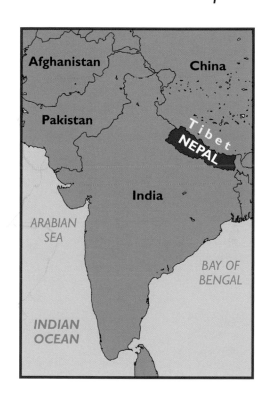

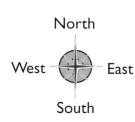

North

West — East

South

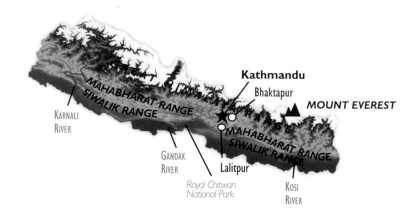

Kathmandu

Bhaktapur

MOUNT EVEREST

GREAT HIMALAYA

MAHABHARAT RANGE

SIWALIK RANGE

KARNALI
RIVER

RANGE

MAHABHARAT RANGE

SIWALIK RANGE

GANDAK
RIVER

Lalitpur

*Royal Chitwan
National Park*

KOSI
RIVER

The Mountain Region is located in northern Nepal. It covers more than half of the country's land. The Great Himalaya Range is part of the Mountain Region. The Great Himalaya Range contains Mount Everest.

Mount Everest

It is the world's highest mountain peak. Mount Everest is located on the border between Nepal and China.

The rivers in Nepal run from north to south. Nepal's major rivers are the Kosi (KOH-see), Gandak (GUHN-duhk), and Karnali (kahr-NAH-lee). They cut through the country's many mountain ranges.

Nepal's climate varies by season. In the winter, the weather is cool and dry. Temperatures quickly rise in the spring. Then in the summer, **monsoons** bring heavy rainfall. The rain gradually ends in the fall.

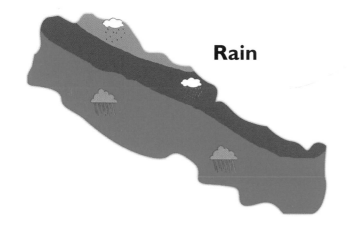

Rain

Rainfall

AVERAGE YEARLY RAINFALL

Inches		*Centimeters*
Under 20		*Under 51*
20 - 59		*51 - 150*
Over 59		*Over 150*

Temperature

AVERAGE TEMPERATURE

Fahrenheit		*Celsius*
Over 68°		*Over 20°*
50° - 68°		*10° - 20°*
32° - 50°		*0° - 10°*
Below 32°		*Below 0°*

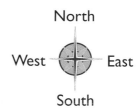

North

West · East

South

Winter

Summer

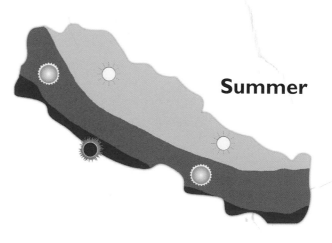

Forests & Flowers

Nepal's land contains many plants. In fact, more than 6,500 types of trees, shrubs, and flowers grow there. These plants vary by altitude.

The Terai region's low, flat land contains forests. A common tree in these forests is the sal. Its hard wood can be used for construction. The Terai also contains evergreens and grasses.

North of the Terai, the land rises and gives way to the Mahabharat Range. This area's most notable plant is the rhododendron (roh-duh-DEHN-druhn). Its red bloom is Nepal's national flower.

This alpine plant has bright, yellow flowers.

Farther north, the land continues to rise until it becomes the Great Himalaya Range. **Alpine** plants grow there. They usually have small, fuzzy leaves and bright flowers.

Hiking is the best way to view the rhododendrons in Nepal.

Saving the Animals

Nepal's land contains a wide variety of animals. They include leopards, tigers, elephants, bears, and deer. More than 800 species of birds and 500 kinds of butterflies live there, too.

Unfortunately, many of Nepal's animals have lost their **habitats**. This happens when people cut down forests. As a result, many of Nepal's animals now live in national parks and reserves.

The one-horned rhinoceros is one of Nepal's endangered species.

Royal Chitwan National Park is Nepal's oldest and best-known national park. It is in the Terai region. Chitwan is famous for its **endangered** animals. They include one-horned rhinoceroses and Royal Bengal tigers.

Axis deer and Hanuman langur monkeys also live in Nepal.

The Nepali People

India and Tibet have had a major effect on Nepal's population. That's because years ago, many Indians and Tibetans migrated to Nepal. Over time, they formed almost 50 distinct groups.

Each group in Nepal has its own style of clothing. However, in the cities men usually wear clothes similar to those worn in the United States and Canada.

Many Nepali purchase food at bazaars.

Women generally wear saris (SAHR-eez) or *kurta*. Saris are dresses that are wrapped and folded. They are usually worn over a blouse. *Kurta* are loose dresses that extend to the ankles. Women wear long pants under their *kurta*.

Examples of traditional and Western clothing styles in Nepal

Two major religions are practiced in Nepal. The majority of Nepali practice **Hinduism**. Other Nepali are **Buddhist**. The founder of Buddhism, Siddhartha Gautama (sihd-DAHR-tuh GOW-tuh-muh), was born in Nepal.

Since most Nepali are **Hindu**, this religion affects Nepal's society. In Hinduism, a **caste** (KAST) system divides people into social classes.

Castes affect everyday life. For example, a person cannot marry someone from a different caste. Similarly, a person cannot eat food prepared by someone of a lower caste.

Hindu Castes

Hinduism has four main castes.

- Priests and scholars
- Rulers and warriors
- Merchants and professionals
- Servants and laborers

Priests and scholars are the highest caste. Servants and laborers are the lowest. A group called the untouchables exists below the lowest caste. The untouchables do jobs none of the castes are allowed to.

In general, Nepali families are large. Men, women, and children all help with farmwork in rural villages. Women also gather firewood, prepare meals, and care for the children. Men tend to family business.

Traditional houses in Nepal are made with brick. **Ornately** carved woodwork surrounds the windows and doors. Nepali homes are usually built around courtyards. Terraces often face the street.

Many Nepali children do not attend school because they are needed to help at home or on the farm.

Nepali children at school

At mealtime, Nepali do not use forks, spoons, or knives. Instead, they eat with their hands. Most of the meals in Nepal are **vegetarian**. A common dish is called *dahl bhaht tarkari*. It consists of rice, vegetables, and lentils.

In Nepal, most people speak Nepali. It is the country's official language. Nepali is based on Sanskrit, which is an ancient Indian language. Besides Nepali, about 12 other languages are spoken in Nepal.

Education in Nepal is improving. Schools are slowly spreading to the country's small villages. Students may attend free government schools. Or, they can pay to attend private schools. Despite these efforts, many Nepali cannot read or write.

Dahl

In Nepali, the word *dahl* means "lentils." Lentils, along with rice and vegetables, are a main part of the Nepali diet.

- 1 pound red lentils
- 1 teaspoon tumeric
- 1 tablespoon corn oil
- 1 teaspoon garlic, minced
- 1 onion, chopped
- 1 teaspoon cumin
- 2 red chilis
- 1 teaspoon coriander

Wash the lentils. In a pan, combine the lentils, six cups of water, a pinch of salt, and tumeric. Heat the mixture for about 20 minutes. Then, remove the pan from the stove. In a different pan, heat the oil and add the remaining ingredients. Once this mixture is well blended, add the lentils. Serve with cooked rice and vegetables.

AN IMPORTANT NOTE TO THE CHEF: Always have an adult help with the preparation and cooking of food. Never use kitchen utensils or appliances without adult permission and supervision.

LANGUAGE

English	Nepali
Hello	Namaste (nuh-muh-STAY)
Please	Kripayah (kree-PUH-yah)
Thanks	Dhanyabad (DHUHN-yuh-buhd)
Yes	Cha (CHUH)
No	Chhaina (CHEYE-nuh)
Okay	Thikcha (TEEK-chuh)

A Nation of Farmers

Farming is the most important part of Nepal's **economy**. Eight out of 10 Nepali work as farmers. They grow enough crops to feed their families. They sell any extra crops for money.

Farmers raise several kinds of crops. Nepal's three most important crops are rice, corn, and wheat. Many farmers also raise livestock. In fact, nearly every farmer owns goats and hens.

This Nepali uses yaks to plow a field.

Most of Nepal's industry is based on farming. Many factories process crops. However, factories also produce other goods. Bricks, tiles, paper, and cement are all made in Nepali factories.

Recently, tourism has become a growing part of Nepal's **economy**. About 300,000 people explore this country each year. They enjoy visiting the ancient temples and hiking across the beautiful land.

Tibetan immigrants began making and selling rugs in Nepal after fleeing Chinese rule in 1959. These rugs are now an important part of Nepal's economy.

Tourists are also drawn to the beautiful rugs made in Nepal. The rugs are a major part of Nepal's economy. People weave them at home or in factories. The rugs are then exported or sold locally.

Old City, New City

Kathmandu is Nepal's capital and largest city. It is located in the eastern half of Nepal, about 65 miles (105 km) north of India. The city is situated in a valley that is surrounded by mountains.

One of Kathmandu's most famous areas is called Durbar Square. It contains more than 50 temples and monuments. Several bazaars are located nearby. There, people can buy everything from yarn to copper pots!

Kathmandu is more than just bazaars and ancient temples. This city also has a new area filled with modern buildings. It is home to the city's banks, restaurants, and other businesses.

The valley that holds Kathmandu also has two other major cities. They are called Lalitpur (luh-LIHT-poor) and Bhaktapur (BUHK-tuh-poor). Like Kathmandu, both of these cities have many ancient religious temples.

The Bodhnath Stupa in Kathmandu is the largest in Nepal. To worship, Buddhists walk clockwise around the stupa's base and spin a prayer wheel located there.

From Here to There

Nepal's transportation system is limited. The country has few roads or cars. As a result, most Nepali travel from place to place by walking. They use trails that cut through Nepal's mountains and valleys.

Animal transportation is also common in Nepal. Nepali ride animals such as elephants, yaks, and donkeys. They also attach carts to bulls, oxen, buffaloes, and horses. The carts can transport people and cargo.

Large animals can travel on terrain that motorized vehicles cannot.

Examples of the front (left) and back of bicycle rickshas

Buses are the main form of public transportation in Nepal. For this reason, they are often crowded. Large cities, such as Kathmandu, also have rickshas (RIHK-shahz). They are carts pulled by either a bicycle or a motorcycle.

Nepal's only international airport is located in Kathmandu. Smaller airports throughout Nepal offer local flights.

Nepal's Government

Nepal's official name is the Kingdom of Nepal. A **monarch**, a **prime minister**, members of **parliament**, and judges form Nepal's government. They must work together to create a country that runs well.

King Gyanendra (right) swore in a new prime minister in October 2002. Lokendra Bahadur Chand will be prime minister until new elections can be held.

Recently, Nepal's government has faced uncertainty. In 2001, the king was murdered. His brother Gyanendra soon took the throne.

In 2002, King Gyanendra dismissed the **prime minister**. He then seized control of the government. Despite this, he says he is committed to keeping Nepal a **democracy**.

King Gyanendra greets his people in June 2001, soon after being crowned king.

Land of Festivals

Nepal is a country brimming with festivals. In fact, Nepali celebrate more than 50 festivals each year. Many of them celebrate **Hindu** gods and goddesses. Others honor the **Buddhist** faith.

Parades are important parts of Nepali festivals.

Dasain is Nepal's biggest festival. It takes place in the fall, and it lasts between 10 and 15 days. Dasain celebrates the Hindu goddess Durga and her victory over evil.

During Dasain, Nepali spend time with their families. Each family sets up an altar to honor Durga. They also sacrifice goats and buffaloes. Parades, dances, and feasts are all part of Dasain, too.

Costumes of animals, gods, and goddesses are worn during Nepal's festivals.

A holiday called Buddha Jayanti honors the founder of **Buddhism**, Siddhartha Gautama. On Gautama's birthday, Buddhists travel to a shrine west of Kathmandu. There, they visit a **stupa** (STOO-puh) and bring offerings to a Buddha statue.

Nepali Culture

Nepal is an ancient nation. Over many years, its people have created a **culture** unlike any other. It is filled with **unique** legends, amazing art, and exciting sports.

One of Nepal's best-known legends is that of the yeti (YEH-tee). According to legend, the yeti is a beast that lives high in the Himalaya. No one has seen the yeti. But, some people think that large footprints found in the snow belong to it.

Temples are examples of Nepal's religious artwork.

This Buddha statue guards the stairs to a Buddhist stupa.

Nepal's **culture** also includes works of art. Artwork in Nepal is often religious. Many temples have **ornate** wood carvings of gods and goddesses. Sculptures of gods and goddesses can also be seen in the hills and around the towns.

Sports are part of Nepal's culture, too. Many Nepali enjoy traditional sports, such as racing on horses. Other popular sports include soccer, volleyball, and table tennis.

Glossary

alpine - of, or relating to growing in the mountains or elevated slopes.

Buddhism - a religion founded in India by Siddhartha Gautama. It teaches that pain and evil are caused by desire. If people have no desire they will achieve a state of happiness called Nirvana.

caste - a social class based on wealth, profession, or occupation.

communist - a person who supports communism. It is a social and economic system in which everything is owned by the government and is distributed to the people as needed.

conquest - the act of conquering.

constitution - the laws that govern a country.

coup - a sudden, violent overthrow of a government by a small group.

culture - the customs, arts, and tools of a nation or people at a certain time.

democracy - a governmental system in which the people vote on how to run their country.

dynasty - a series of rulers who belong to the same family.

economy - the way a nation uses its money, goods, and natural resources.

endangered - in danger of becoming extinct.

habitat - a place where a living thing is naturally found.

Hinduism - a religion of India. It emphasizes dharma, or the principles of existence, and its rituals and ceremonies.

isolate - to separate from other nations, societies, or peoples.

monarchy - a government ruled by a king or queen.

monsoon - a seasonal wind that sometimes brings heavy rain.

ornate - elaborately detailed decoration.

parliament - the highest lawmaking body of some governments.

prime minister - the highest-ranked member of some governments.

rebel - one who disobeys an authority or the government.

stupa - a dome-shaped Buddhist shrine.

unique - being the only one of its kind.

vegetarian - a meal that does not contain meat.

Web Sites

To learn more about Nepal, visit ABDO Publishing Company on the World Wide Web at **www.abdopub.com**. Web sites about the country are featured on our Book Links page. These links are routinely monitored and updated to provide the most current information available.

Index